How To Keep The Kids From Moving Back In!

By MARTIN A. RAGAWAY

Illustrations By DON ROBB

Tell your daughter you've become a
transvestite and you may be borrowing
her clothes from time to time.

a **Laughter Library** book

PRICE/STERN/SLOAN
Publishers, Inc., Los Angeles

1986

THIRD PRINTING — JANUARY 1986

Copyright© 1984 by the Laughter Library
Published by Price/Stern/Sloan Publishers, Inc.
410 North La Cienega Boulevard, Los Angeles, California 90048

ISBN: 0-8431-0990-4

Stick it to them. Put honey on the doorknobs.

Sell off every part of the house except one bedroom.

When you put out the cornflakes
in the morning also put out a jar of
tenderizer.

Become super moralistic.
Make your daughter and her
husband sleep in separate bedrooms.

Switch the labels on the tubes of Preparation H
and Crazy Glue.

Hide hemlock leaves
in his stash
of marijuana.

Pretend to be absent-
minded. Keep leaving your
dentures in the tuna salad.

Have the family physician call and ask when they're coming in for their distemper shots.

Start off every sentence with, "Now, when I was your age, I..."

Put a sign on the pool:

Follow them around with a pooper-scooper.

Warn them, "If you don't eat all your peas, you don't get dessert," and then give them a pair of chopsticks.

Tell them you're happy to have them home and you're sure they won't mind sharing a closet with your vampire bats.

In his bathroom: Put a toothbrushing chart with stars.

Send them on an all expense-paid trip on a slowboat to China.

You hesitate kicking them out
because you're afraid they'll write
a book about how you abused
them when they were kids.

Give the clothes they intend to inherit to
Goodwill — accidentally.

Borrow his car and return it
with the gas tank empty.

Use her manicure scissors to strip tv antenna wire.

Serve boiled fish six nights in a row and on the seventh night, switch to beef liver and lima beans.

Explain there isn't enough time for everyone in the bathroom. Make her go out in the garage and shower with the Water Pik.

Cook your special recipe for codfish balls and put in **extra** bones.

Put selected and suggestive books in his room such as:

HOW I MADE A MILLION
SMUGGLING COKE OUT OF
COLUMBIA.

Nag at them, constantly. "I want
something for you that you never
had as a child. A clean room."

How to tell the kids have
returned: Count the open
soda cans in the fridge.

Put the phone bill in their names.

Put a school of piranha in the Jacuzzi.

Make them wipe their feet
before leaving the house so
they won't track dirt all over
the neighborhood.

Save your poor taste, dirty jokes to tell
their dates.

Encourage woodpeckers to nest in their headboard.

Tell her that she's adopted. That her real parents dropped her on your doorstep and ran away. If that doesn't work, present her a bill covering food and rent for the first 20 years.

Keep them off balance. If they ask, "What happened to our dog?" You say, "Shut up and eat your cat."

Nominate your son-in-law as
Grand Marshal in the Gay Day Parade.

Put up a sign:

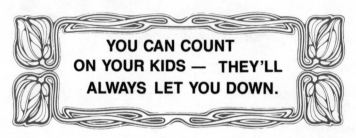

**YOU CAN COUNT
ON YOUR KIDS — THEY'LL
ALWAYS LET YOU DOWN.**

Tell him the library called.
He owes $3,500 in
overdue book fines
and the police are coming
out with a warrant
for his arrest.

Use their expensive stereo
turntable as a potter's wheel.

Leave them there and you
run away from home.

Straighten up her room so she can't find anything.

Let them borrow your
Scrabble set but hide the vowels.

Find what books they're reading and constantly change the bookmark.

Leave travel folders of Hawaii, New Zealand and Australia around their room.

Use his electric razor to trim the hedge.

Make them keep the same curfew hours they had when they were 12.

Tell your daughter you've become a transvestite and you may be borrowing her clothes from time to time.

Take the door off the bathroom.

Drop bits of philosophy whenever you can, such as: "You know life doesn't really begin until all the kids are out of the house and the dog dies."

Go to a masquerade party as Minnie Mouse and use her falsies as ears.

Never get involved with her problems. No matter what.

How do I know who the father is? You never let me go steady.

Now, at bedtime, you say *your* prayers. That they move out in the middle of the night.

If she's expecting guests always go to the front door with your fly open.

Eat all the ice cream in the carton except one spoonful and then put it back in the freezer.

Put in a coin operated coffee machine.

When they ask if you missed
them while they were gone say,
"No, they opened an aggravation
parlor downtown and they
deliver."

For breakfast, serve
oatmeal that has
to be cut
with a knife.

He was raised with a dog in the house so he could learn about love and good manners. Now, you've got a dog that eats with the right fork and a kid who goes out on the lawn and chases cars.

Get into cryogenics. If an elderly aunt dies, have her body frozen so when they go down to the kitchen for a midnight snack, she falls out of the freezer.

Set fire to the welcome mat and throw it in his room.

Drop little hints at the dinner table like: "Children and parents should never be in the same family."

Put Super Glue on a Lawrence Welk cassette and jam it in their car stereo.

For breakfast, serve pancakes that are Scotch Taped together.

Show them who's boss. Insist
they recycle the toothpaste
by putting the extra back in the tube.

Hang some mistletoe on the front door
so they'll be constantly reminded that when
they move back you kissed your trip to
Europe goodbye.

Clean a chicken in her bathroom.

Make him feel unwelcome whenever you can. On his birthday, remind him that he caused you morning sickness. AFTER he was born.

Simonize his bathtub.

Xerox her date book and send a copy to everyone on her Christmas list.

You know the kids have
moved back in when the dog
answers to you, you answer
to your wife and your
children answer to nobody.

Put a sign in their room:
AMERICAN EXPRESS
WELCOME HERE.

Pay extra attention to them. While cleaning
house, dust and wax them.

Remind him how he tried to run away when
he was six years old and you stopped him.
Now, offer to drive him down to the
Greyhound Bus Station.

Give his favorite blazer a little individuality.

Put a tv camera in their bedroom and have it scan every 20 seconds.

Start a black widow spider colony in her underwear drawer.

Tell them you're delighted to have them back home and he's lucky you saved his furniture.

Go to the post office and fill out a
change of address card so they won't
get their unemployment insurance checks.

Invite a different dinner guest
every night. All the boys you think your
daughter **should** have married.

Dress younger than they do.

Make his friends your friends.
Make as many of them as you can.

Tell them that since you expect
them to help clean, you just fired
the housekeeper.

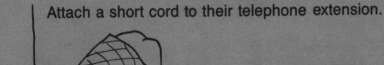
Attach a short cord to their telephone extension.

Put a sign in the garage:

> DO NOT USE CAR
> UNLESS YOU KNOW
> HOW TO DEFUSE A BOMB.

Try to get them interested in your new hobby — finger painting with bat guano.

Tell him you're really gay. "I only came out of the closet once — about nine months before you were born."

Start raising carp in your hot tub.

Run movies of his third birthday party.

Buy cheap toilet paper. The kind where you can't tell where the roll starts.

Do not ask for whom the bell tolls. You'll know when you get the phone bill.

Fill his water bed with
gasoline and put up a sign:

SMOKING PERMITTED.

Sneak in while they are asleep
and snip off half his mustache.
And glue it on her.

Put mousetraps in the cookie jar
where the money used to be.

Loan them credit cards which
you've already reported as stolen.

Display a
cat-o-nine tails
in the living room
and tell them
it's never too late
for child beating.

No reflection on her, but remove every mirror in the house.

Put skunk musk in her hair dryer.

When you have a sit-down dinner party, make them eat at a card table in the hallway.

Invite the teacher who flunked him in algebra to move into the guest room.

Put in a coin operated washer and dryer.

Father to daughter and son-in-law:
When I told you to save money where
ever you can, I didn't mean hitchhike to
our house for dinner every night.

If their room has color tv,
computer, stereo, refrigerator,
change rooms with them
immediately.

Fold up the hide-a-bed while they are
in it and yell "tornado."

Never miss a chance to zap
in a zinger. If he comes to
the door and says, "Is that
dinner I smell?" you say, "It
is and you do."

Put the stereo on an all-Wagner radio station.
Take off the tuning knob and hide it.

Nag! Nag! Nag!
Remind them once a day how
much it cost to put them through
college — but it was worth it.
They still can't get a job but at
least they know which field it's in.

Put wire hangers in their closet and
reverse every other one.

Take in her skirts a quarter o
an inch a day, so she'll think
she's putting on weight.

Pretend to be hard of hearing. Make them
repeat everything twice.

Try bribes. Offer to resume her weekly allowance. Better than that, if she moves out you'll double it.

Do a needlepoint. Hang it up in his room.

Give them a feeling of insecurity. Call a house moving company for bids on just moving one room.

Hold a garage sale in her old room.

Borrow his clothes. Tell him
you're into wearing hand-me-ups

Decorate their room to make it
look just like a Roach Motel.

Put a bumper sticker on his car:

ALL COPS ARE RIDICULOUSLY
OVERPAID

Put some vanishing cream in her
bathroom. Some real vanishing cream.

In the middle of the night, sneak into his room and pour
a cup of warm lemonade under his covers.

Lick all the frosting off their
Oreo cookies. Put them back
in the package.

Establish an 11 o'clock
lock out.
Not only that,
pull up the drawbridge.

Help her to save money by sewing
clothes at home and while you're at it
make an exact duplicate for yourself.

Put burlap towels in her bathroom.

Use his stamp collection to
mail your Christmas cards.

Tell the kids that since they moved back home, you're considering something you never thought of before. A divorce.

Put a lock on the refrigerator door.

Try staying out all night. Don't call and tell them where you are.

Show friends her nude baby pictures.

Run all the hot water
whenever she takes a shower.

Cook exotic dishes like pork tartar.

Buy him a hunting outfit and take him out to shoot deer.

It's impossible to love the same child for 20 years. (After 20 years, it's not the same child.)

Grown-up kids are like winter storms. They may be late, but they never fail to show up.

Consider yourself a successful parent if they flip off the headlights before turning into the driveway at four in the morning.

Now that the kids are back, you don't have to eat leftovers. There aren't any.

Remember when you worried because you didn't know where your children were. Now, you do. They're back in their own rooms.

When children return to the family home, it's a gesture of reciprocal love. You drove them to school and now they're driving you up the wall.

PARENTS WHOSE
OVED BACK IN.

Until they moved back home you never knew
what cramped quarters meant.

You can't reason with them and you can't hit
them. How did they get so big and strong on
junk food?

Why did they have to return just when
everything started to click for you? Your
teeth, your knees, your back.

It isn't aimed at you, personally. When
newlyweds can't scratch up enough chicken
feed to feather their own nest, they come
home and pluck their parents.

You never realize what a happy marriage
you've had until the kids move back — and
then it's too late.

Before they left, the kids were deductible.
Now, they're just taxing.